# ISTANBUL

BONECHI & NET

ISTANBUL
*Publication created and designed by:* Casa Editrice Bonechi
*Photographic research:* Serena de Leonardis
*Graphic and layout:* Serena de Leonardis

*Text:* Giovanna Magi *and* Rita Bianucci
*English translation:* Studio Comunicare, Firenze
*Editing:* Simonetta Giorgi
*Drawing on page 40:* Stefano Benini
*Map of Istanbul:* a courtesy of NET

*The cover, layout and artwork by Casa Editrice Bonechi*
*graphic artists in this publication are protected by international copyright.*
Photographs from the archives of Casa Editrice Bonechi taken by Luigi Di Giovine *(pages 13, 14, 16 bottom, 17 top, 25 bottom, 34, 36 bottom, 42 top, 43 top, 56, 57, 58, 59, 60, 62 bottom, 75, 80, 83 bottom, 84, 85, 89, 101, 103 bottom, 111, 112)* and Paolo Giambone *(pages 11, 27, 70 top, 71 bottom, 73, 74, 78, 79, 81 top and bottom right, 82, 83 top, 88, 107, 108, 109 left).*
Photographs on pages 3, 5, 6/7, 8/9, 10, 16 top, 17 bottom, 18, 19, 20 left, 21 top, 22, 23, 24, 25 top, 28, 29 bottom, 32, 33, 36 top, 37, 38, 39, 42 centre, 42 bottom, 43 bottom, 46, 52, 53, 61, 62 top, 63, 65, 67 bottom, 68, 69, 70 centre, 70 bottom, 71 top, 72, 76, 77, 81 bottom left, 86, 87, 90, 91, 92, 93, 96, 97, 98, 99, 100, 102, 103 top, 104, 105, 106, 109 right, 110, 113, 114/115, 116/117, 118, 119, 120, 121, 122/123, 124, 125 were kindly supplied by NET.
Photographs on pages 4, 12, 15 bottom right, 21 bottom, 26, 27 top, 30, 31, 40/41, 44, 45, 64, 66/67, 94, 95 are by Gianni Dagli Orti.

**ISBN 88-8029-225-0**

* * *

# BYZANTIUM, CONSTANTINOPLE, ISTANBUL: THE STORY OF A CITY

*I stanbul: a key point in world geography, focal point of the interests of international powers, capital of an empire, the only city in the world that belongs to two continents – Europe and Asia. Its origins are lost in the mists of time and have become legend. The story is told of a group of Doric colonists from Megara who landed and settled on the Asian coast of the Bosphorus and founded a colony at Chalcedon. In 658 B. C. a second group of colonists led by king Byzas decided to consult the oracle of Delphi before starting out on their trip. The oracle advised them to stop on the land «across from the land of the blind». The sagacious interpretation of Byzas led him to found a colony on the European shores opposite Chalcedon, in a peaceful sheltered port, whereas the precedent colonists, in their blindness, had been unable to appreciate the beauty of the spot and had preferred a wind-swept*

*bay. The place Byzas chose was actually the best of all possible places with a highly strategic position. Indeed through the strait of the Bosphorus the Black Sea communicates with the Sea of Marmara which in turn empties into the Aegean through the strait of the Dardanelles and then into the Mediterranean. «The ocean surrounds Constantinople like a garland» wrote Procopius. And it is at this specific point that the Bosphorus forms a long winding natural port in the shape of an ox horn, known as the Golden Horn. Thanks to its position, Byzantium soon became an important trading center and was coveted by her greedy neighbors. The first of these was Darius of Persia, who conquered the city in 513 B. C. Freed by Pausanius of Sparta, Byzantium tenaciously resisted Philip of Macedon, Alexander the Great's father, who besieged the city in 340 B. C. The story goes that one night the moon suddenly*

3

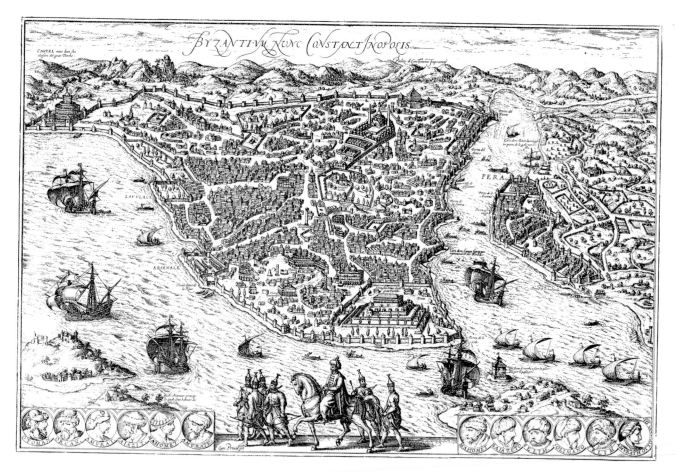

Osman Hamdy Bey (1842-1910): the Mausoleum of Sehzade.

Istanbul city plan by Giovanni Vavassore, 1520.

came out from behind the clouds, revealing the imminent enemy attack to the Byzantines. Ever since, the crescent moon has become a symbol of the city. After having entered into an alliance with the Romans, the city made the mistake of siding with Pescennius Niger, an adversary of Septimius Severus who razed the city to the ground in 196 A. D. after a long siege. Despite this, Septimius Severus was just and generous and rebuilt the city, constructing theaters, baths, the hippodrome and giving it a Latin name, Augusta Antonia, in honor of his son Antoninus who was to become emperor under the name of Caracalla. In the third century A. D. while Rome, weakened by the continuous barbarian invasions, was inexorably on the wane, the star of Byzantium was growing ever brighter. In 324 A. D. Constantine reunited the two parts of the Empire and on May 11, 330, he solemnly consecrated the city as the new capital with the name of Nea Roma or New Rome. It was however to be known as Constantinople and while the Latin culture found itself in a state of crisis the road was paved for the creation of a new and original culture which characterized the Byzantine civilization and which was to shine for centuries. Like Rome, Constantinople spread its walls over seven hills. It reached the apex of its splendor under the Emperor Justinian, sole head of State and Church, after the sun of the

Roman Empire of the West had definitely set. The official language was no longer Latin but Greek and the emperor assumed the title of «basileus». Paradoxically, it was Costantinople's Latin heritage which began to undermine its foundations. After having wrenched political power from Rome, Costantinople also wanted religious supremacy. The eternal conflict between the East and the West had already been exacerbated by the iconoclastic controversy and was now to deteriorate as a result of the series of excommunications which the two empires issued against each other. At the end of the 11th century the spiritual tension present in the West together with the idea of liberating the holy places in Jerusalem from the infidels led to the institution of the Crusades. While the first three crusades were based on religious inspiration, this was hardly true of the fourth crusade. The personal interests of Venice as opposed to the Eastern Empire, the spirit of adventure and conquest on the part of the knights, the mirage of the wealth which had accumulated in the capital, distracted the crusaders from their original «noble» concept.

In April of 1204 the Christian knights conquered Constantinople where they plundered and killed without pity, pillaging and destroying. Countless priceless treasures were melted down or were lost. With no more than a hundred thousand inhabitants,

5

*The Blue Mosque.*

and completely lacking its past splendor, Constantinople was reconquered by the Byzantine Empire in 1261, with a fortuitous bloodless surprise attack. The new Paleologue dynasty had to keep its own between the numerous intestine struggles and the ever-growing external pressure of the Ottoman Turks. The irresistible rise of Ottoman power began in 1451 when the able and ambitious sultan Mohammed II ascended the throne. His only dream had always been to take over Costantinople. The young sultan had about 80,000 men against the 200,000 of the emperor Constantine XI Paleologue. Juggernaut of the Turkish army was a corps of fanatic soldiers that were highly devoted to the sultan and were called «janissaries» (from the Turkish word Yeni-ceri which means «new troops»), the descendants of Christian minorities which had been converted to Islam. The confidence of the Turkish army was based on an ancient Islamic prophesy which said «Constantinople will be conquered: glory to the prince and the army which will accomplish the enterprise».The siege began on April 5, 1453. The Byzantines had blocked the Golden Horn with floating tree trunks and the Turkish fleet was unable to force the blockade. The sultan then commanded his troops to drag about 70 ships across the peninsula of Pera, moving them on wagons and wooden tracks. The chronicles of the time narrate that it was «an extraordinary sight to see these ships, with their sails battened, their crews and their equipment, slide through the fields as if they were in the open seas». In order to launch their final attack, the Turks built a bridge of barrels which united their camp with the mainland. From here the

Following pages: the Blue Mosque facing Hagia Sophia.

*Turkish artillery soon shattered the fortifications which Theodosius II had erected in the 5th century. At half past one, the morning of May 29th, the Turks overran the conquered city and the ensuing destruction made no distinction between men and things. Christian Constantinople thus ended up in the hands of a sultan who was little more than 23 years old. Later the new city was to have another name, Istanbul, an abbreviated form of the Greek expression «eis ten polin» which means «towards the City». Generous with the vanquished, Mohammed II (who from then on was to be called Fatih, the Conqueror), guaranteed their old privileges to the Genovese and the Venetians, opened his court to artists and scholars of all races and religions, left freedom of worship to the Greeks and the Armenians. As a result of the sultan's tolerance*

*many Christians settled in Istanbul. The Ottoman empire reached the zenith of its power under Suleyman I known as the Magnificent by Westerners and as the Lawmaker by the Turks. His great architect Sinan adorned the city with grand mosques, bridges, palaces and fountains. Istanbul was at the same time the capital of Islam for the sultan was also Caliph, that is the spiritual leader of the Muslims. The history of the city is inseparable from that of the empire, sharing in its vicissitudes, suffering its fate. As the Ottoman power gradually waned and the empire was dismembered, the city too declined until the dawn of the 20th century saw the end of the empire and the birth of the young Turkish republic. In 1923 the capital was transferred to Ankara, but the history of its millennial past lives on in the glorious monuments of Istanbul.*

7

No one who has been to Istanbul at least once can ever forget the feeling of awe and wonder inspired by the sight of the slender minarets boldly silhouetted against the sky, the looming bulk, the cascade of domes and half domes, the astonishing harmony of its colors and forms. The view is incomparable either from Galata Bridge or from the Golden Horn. Sultan Ahmed's mosque stands firmly opposite Hagia Sophia as if it were trying to rival it in size and grandeur.

Sultan Ahmed I, who came to the throne when he was barely fourteen, was deeply religious and entrusted the construction to a pupil of the great Sinan, the architect Mohammed Ağa, known also as «Sedefkâr», which means «worker of mother-of-pearl». According to a manuscript in the Topkapı library he was originally a gardener in the mausoleum of Süleyman's mosque. He had joined the Janissaries and had dedicated himself to the building of mosques, palaces and fountains, even going so far as to restore the Kaaba.

Work on the mosque began in 1609 and ended in 1616, just a year before the death of the sultan who had spent 1,181 gold thalers on it. It is said that on the day of the solemn inauguration Ahmed I, as a sign of humility, wore a hat in the shape of the Prophet's foot.

The first thing that strikes us as we approach the mosque is that it is the only one in the world to have six minarets, four of which have three balconies each. When the building was finished, the sultan had to add a seventh minaret to the mosque of the Mecca which also had six in order to reestablish its religious primacy.

The mosque is surrounded on three sides by a vast walled courtyard with a portico. Three impressive entrance doors lead into an internal court, paved in marble, which is as large as the inside of the

*Two views of the Blue Mosque.*

The Blue Mosque seen from the inner courtyard.

The vast interior of the Blue Mosque, with its imposing grooved pillars.

mosque. In the center of the court is the hexagonal *Şadirvan* (basin or fountain for ritual ablutions) surrounded by six marble columns.

The inside is approximately square. Mohammed Ağa, following the example set by his master Sinan, eliminated the separation between the nave and side aisles, creating a single immense space into which the light pours from 260 windows, freely playing over the surfaces. The powerful dome, 43 meters high, is supported by four enormous circular pillars 5 meters in diameter which have vertical grooves and are known as «elephant feet».

The mosque takes its name from the splendid blue decoration which covers this perfectly balanced harmonious ensemble. For a third of their height the walls and pillars are sheathed with 21,043 faience tiles of the 16th and 17th centuries, predominantly in all possible shades of blue and with floral designs ranging from roses to tulips, carnations and lilacs. The *mimbar* (pulpit), stylistically similar to the one in the Mecca, and the *mihrab* (prayer niche indicating the direction of Mecca), which preserves a fragment of the black stone of the Kaaba and is decorated with precious stones, are both of pure white marble.

*A view of the interior of the Mosque with the white marble pulpit (mimbar) and the prayer niche (mihrab) oriented towards Mecca*

*Two views of the inner dome.*

*The interior of the Mosque, with the worshippers at prayer.*

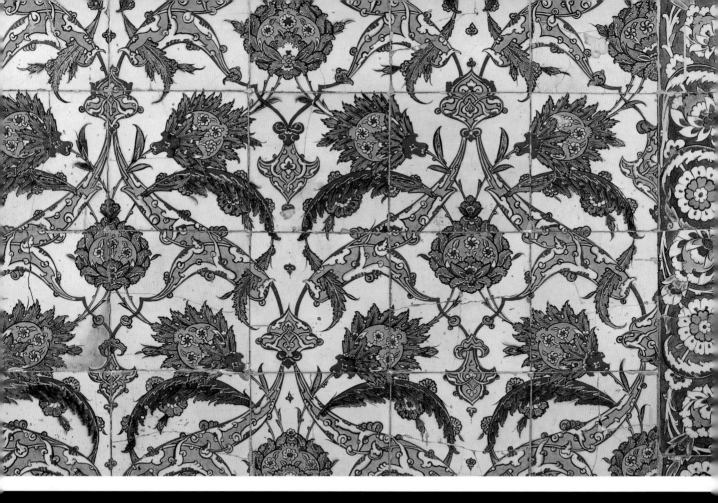

*A detail of the ceramic tiles in the Blue Mosque.*

*The Blue Mosque at night.*

*The Kaiser Fountain.*

*The 16th century Double Baths (Çifte Hamam) located between Hagia Sophia Museum and the Blue Mosque.*

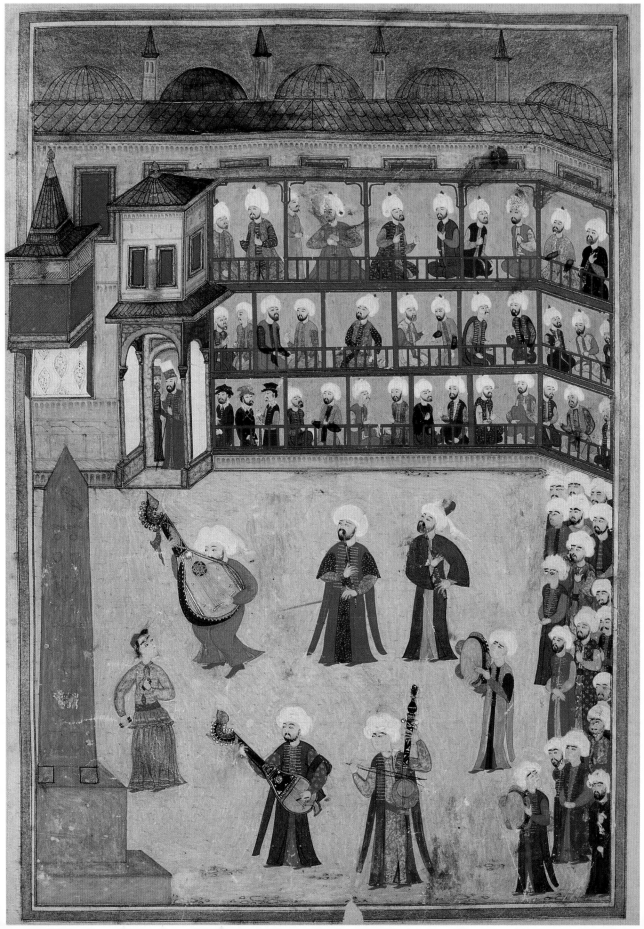

The vast area covered by the Hippodrome lies between Hagia Sophia and the Blue Mosque. It is also known as At Meydani, or plaza of the horses, because after the conquest of Constantinople it was used principally for horse races. Its original layout dates to 203 A. D. under Septimius Severus. It was enlarged and embellished by Constantine in 325 and recalls the Circus Maximus in Rome. Almost 400 meters long and 120 meters wide there was room for 100,000 spectators in forty rows of seats. The athletes were divided into four factions: the Blues, the Greens, the Reds, and the Whites. The emperor's box, decorated with four splendid bronze horses which are now in Venice, was to the north. But the plaza of the horses was not the scene of games and festivities only. In 532, during the Ides of January, the revolt against Justinian was staged here. At the cry of nika (which in Greek means «victory»), the rebels raged through the city pillaging and plundering.

The uprising, which went down in history as the Nika riots, was bloodily put down by General Belisarius who had over 40,000 men executed next to what was known from then on as the «gate of death». In 1826 the Hippodrome was once more the scene for the execution of 30,000 Janissaries who had opposed the rule of Sultan Mahmud II.

The Hippodrome was so resplendent with statues, obelisks and trophies which came from various countries that St. Jerome wrote: «the splendor of Constantinople is inaugurated despoiling all other cities».

*A 16th century miniature showing a ceremony of the musicians in front of the Ibrahim Paşa Palace in the Hippodrome.*

*A view of the Hippodrome and Hagia Sophia in the background.*

The oldest is without doubt the *obelisk of Theodosius,* a porphyry monolith 25 meters high from Karnak where it had been erected in honor of Thutmosis III. The marble base is 6 meters high and is decorated with bas-reliefs. Another obelisk is that of Constantine, better known as the *walled obelisk,* which is compared to the Colossus of Rhodes in the inscription on its base. It is 32 meters high and is built of blocks of limestone faced with plaques of gilded bronze and was erected under Constantine VII Porphyrogenitus. The oddest monument is without doubt the *Serpentine Column,* originally 8 meters high (today five and a half meters are left). This bronze column came from Delphi where it had been set up in the temple of Apollo in memory of the victorious battles of Salamis and Platea. It is said that the bodies of the three entwined serpents which form the column were cast from the shields of the Persian soldiers who fell in battle.

Lastly the *Kaiser fountain,* a gift of the German emperor William II to Sultan Abdülhamid II in 1895, during the Kaiser's trip to the East.

*A view of the obelisk of Theodosius and three details of its base.*

# MUSEUM OF TURKISH AND ISLAMIC ARTS

Since 1983, the museum has occupied the 16th century building situated along the western side of Sultanahmet Square (the Hippodrome). The building used to be the palace of Ibrahim Paşa. Apart from the imperial palaces, it is the only extant private palace. The edifice surrounds the three sides of a terrace, forming a courtyard in the middle.

Following the entrance, the first section of the museum is reached by a staircase from the courtyard. Rare ancient works of art created in various Islamic lands are on display in the hallways and in the rooms. Stone and baked clay objects, ceramic and glassware, and handwritten books are some of the most valuable examples of their period. The carpets exhibited in the large halls occupying the section of the building with wide windows in the facade, are magnificent examples of the famous 13th-20th century hand-knotted Turkish carpets. This matchless collection is the richest of its kind in the world. The 13th century Seljouk carpets and rare examples from the following centuries are restored and exhibited with much care.

*The Museum of Turkish and Islamic Arts: the wooden case of the Koran.*

*A partial view of the Museum of Turkish and Islamic Arts.*

# MUSEUM OF CARPETS AND KILIMS

The Administration of Pious Foundations of the Turkish Republic owns an extensive collection of old carpets and kilims, but only a part of this collection is displayed.

The carpets are exhibited in the Sultan's Pavilion in the Sultanahmet Mosque, and the kilims in the vaulted lower galleries entered through the rear gardens of the mosque. The best examples of 13th-20th century Turkish carpets are exhibited along the ramp which is the entrance to the pavilion, and in the rooms where the Sultan used to rest. The carpets and kilims on display have been restored and are displayed in a contemporary fashion.

*An interior view of the Museum of Carpets and Kilims: display room.*

*The Gürdes carpet (18th century).*

*The Konya-Ladik carpet (18th century).*

The marketplace behind the Sultanahmet Mosque is situated on the remains of an old palace dated between the 4th and 6th centuries. The mosaics of the palace were discovered at the lower edge of the market, in their original places. It is known that these mosaics, unearthed in the 1930s, used to decorate the floor of a large hall in the palace. Various hunting scenes from everyday life and impressive decorative designs exhibit high quality workmanship. Buds encircled by bent acanthus leaves, a Medusa head and scenes from a lion hunt are some of the most attractive examples. Scenes depicted by these mosaic panels, created in the style of Antakya Mosaic School (Roman Age), are extremely realistic. Following the discovery of these mosaics, other mosaics unearthed in other sections of the city were framed by concrete panels and brought here to be displayed. Restoration of the market place has been completed and the Mosaic Museum has been reopened to the public.

*Mosaics from the Grand Byzantine Royal Palace: details of a camel ride (left) and a bear devouring a stag (below).*

*Mosaics from the Grand Byzantine Royal Palace: head of Dyonisus (right) and a tiger hunt (below).*

Hagia Sophia or the Church of Divine Wisdom is a masterpiece of grandeur and proportions, coveted by the Islamic East and the Christian West, and one of the most important attestations of humanity – surely the only one that for 1400 years has served God and Allah, the Christian world and Islam. «A spectacle of prodigious beauty, it rises up to defy the heavens themselves», so wrote the Byzantine historian Procopius more than 14 centuries ago.

The first church was built between 325 and 360 under Constans II, even though his father Constantine may have had the foundations laid. Ravaged by fire in 404, it was restored and reconsecrated by Theodosius II only to be completely burnt down during the Nika riots in January 532. Justinian had only recently risen to the throne and the supreme ambition of the emperor, a champion of the cause of orthodox Christianity and divinely appointed, was to build the greatest temple that Christianity had ever had. No more than 32 days had elapsed after the destruction of the church when work on the new building began. It is said that the shape of the church was revealed to Justinian in a dream.

Artisans arrived from all parts of the world. Justinian, who spent much of his time in the building yards, named one hundred overseers each one responsible for a hundred workers. Anthemios of Tralles was designated as architect in chief, assisted by Isidoros of Miletos, both Greeks from Asia Minor. On December 27, 537, Hagia Sophia was solemnly consecrated by the emperor who came out of his palace in all his pomp and ceremony after having sacrificed to God a thousand oxen, six thousand sheep and six hundred deer. Nor had he forgotten the needy, to whom he distributed 30,000 bushels of grain. It is said that when he arrived in front of the church, Justinian raised his arms to heaven and exclaimed «Glory to God who has deigned to let me finish so great a work. O Solomon, I have outdone thee!». And indeed Hagia Sophia seems to surpass Solomon's temple in size, beauty and richness. The use of wood was prohibited for fear of fire. Porphyry came from the quarries of Thebes in Egypt and green marble from Thessaly and columns from the temple of Artemis in Ephesos and the temple of the sun in Baalbek. The grand in-

*Hagia Sophia: the dome.*

*Hagia Sophia and the vast square in front of it.*

*Hagia Sophia: the interior.*

terior of the basilica is central plan. With a total surface of 7,570 square meters, Hagia Sophia takes fourth place after St. Peter's, the Cathedral of Seville and that of Milan. The interior is dominated by the enormous dome 55 meters above the ground and with a diameter of over 36 meters. Forty ribs divide the dome into sections which terminate at their base in 40 windows. The weight of the dome is supported by four main pillars which in turn are buttressed by four smaller pillars. According to Procopius, lime was not used at all, only limestone together with melted lead which was poured into the interstices where it spread and solidified thus closing the joints. Hagia Sophia was also an exultation of light which entered through the numerous windows to illuminate the nave where the worshippers were gathered in prayer. A large metal ring bearing silver plates with oil lamps was suspended from the dome by long chains. At night thousands of lamps and candelabra reflected their light on the 16,000 square meters of gold mosaics scattered here and there throughout the building. At the time these mosaics were made by inserting glass cubes on which gold or silver leaf had been applied into the moist plaster. The dome too was covered by a pure gold mosaic, with a cross at the center. Unfortunately most of the mosaic decoration of Hagia Sophia disappeared, first under the wrath of the iconoclasts, who spared only the abstract decoration, and subsequently with the conquest of the Ottoman Turks and the Islamic prohibition to reproduce the human figure. Natural calamities sorely tried the architectural challenge of Hagia Sophia. The earthquakes of 553 and 557 weakened the structure of the basilica, until in 558 the eastern arch and part of the dome crashed to the ground destroying the altar, the ciborium and the ambo. Restored and newly consecrated, Hagia Sophia was to see other more tragic events. At the

*Virgin and Child between emperors Justinian and Constantine.*

*The lovely 12th century mosaic of the deësis in the south gallery. The Virgin and St. John the Baptist interceding with Christ.*

The Virgin flanked by the Emperor John II Comnenus and
his wife Eirene.

Christ, detail of the mosaic of the deësis in the
south gallery.

Christ Pantocrator flanked by the Empress Zoë and her
husband Constantine IX Monomachus.

Between 1847 and 1849 Gaspare Fossati replaced the sultan's loggia built by Ahmed III with this exagonal one in marble.

The columns and the arches of the gallery.

beginning of the 13th century Constantinople, after having withstood at least seventeen sieges by barbarians and infidels, fell under the fury of a Christian army. During the three days of plunder, Hagia Sophia was completely pillaged and stripped of its precious icons, its gold and silver candelabra, the jeweled crosses, the glittering reliquaries. Anything of gold was simply melted down. In the following centuries, particularly after the reconquest of the city by the Byzantine Empire, Hagia Sophia was partially restored but the general decline of the city, of the dynasty and of the entire empire had inevitably begun. The state of total abandon the city had fallen into facilitated the conquest of Constantinople by the Ottoman Turks on May 29, 1453. That day, late in the afternoon, Mohammed II entered Hagia Sophia and for the first time after nine centuries, the imam's prayer to Allah, the only god, resounded under the imposing domes. This time too there was enormous destruction but it was nothing compared to what had happened 250 years

before. The transformation of Hagia Sophia into a mosque was carried out with unbelievable respect, even though there were of course many changes. The metal cross on the dome was replaced by the crescent moon which a century later was covered – it is said – with 50,000 fused gold coins. The ambo was replaced by a mimbar and a mihrab for prayer in the direction of Mecca was set up. An initial polygonal minaret was built to which others were later added. But the icons, the iconostasis, and various Christian mosaics with human figures were not touched. In addition, the magnificent architecture of the church with its imposing dome and enormous size served as a prototype for the numerous mosques which the new conquerors began to build.
The exterior of Hagia Sophia was also modified. What had been the baptistery was transformed at the beginning of the 17th century into the turbeh of Mustafa I, where this sultan is buried together with his nephew Ibrahim. Next to this mausoleum are the octagonal and hexagonal tombs of three other sul-

*Mausoleum of Selim II, the sultan who was defeated in 1571 by the Venetian and Spanish fleets in the famous battle of Lepanto*

tans, Mohammed III, Selim II and Murat III, each with their wives and relatives.

From the middle of the 18th century on, however, even the surviving mosaics were whitewashed and at the end of the 18th century, from the point of view of decoration and structure, Hagia Sophia was in a state of abandon, the result of natural calamities and the indifference of man. In 1846 two Swiss brothers, Giuseppe and Gaspare Fossati, were called in by the sultan Abdülmecid to restore the church. The two architects had to demolish all the buildings which had sprung up around the mosque throughout the centuries so they could properly shore it up. As for the mosaics, they were gradually uncovered, described, drawn, and then covered over again. This was the last important restoration of Hagia Sophia. The 20th century brought the downfall of the Ottoman Empire and the simultaneous rise of the young Turkish republic.

The first president, Kemal Atatürk, decided to transform the mosque into a Byzantine-Ottoman museum and in April 1932 the mosaics once more began to be laid bare.

Despite the problems involved in removing the whitewash without harming the mosaic, under the careful guidance of Thomas Whittemore of the Byzantine Institute of America the gleaming gold mosaics began to surface from the walls of the mosque, direct evidence of the great past of Hagia Sophia and of the city as a whole.

# THE MAUSOLEUM OF SULTAN SELIM II

After completing his masterpiece, the Selimiye Mosque, Sinan the Architect then constructed the tomb of Selim II, the most beautiful of these polygonal mausoleums in Istanbul. While still alive, Sultan Selim II ordered Sinan to undertake the reinforcement of the buttresses of Hagia Sophia Mosque, the addition of two minarets, and the construction of a tomb for the sultan alongside the mosque. When the sultan died in 1574 however the tomb was not as yet completed. After the funeral ceremonies were over, work on the construction of the tomb continued and the structure was finished in 1577.

The building is octagonal in shape and its exterior is faced entirely in marble. The angles at four of the corners were made wider than the other four, thus providing the structure with a distinctive look. The portico on the front possesses a magnificent appearance. Above the marble inscriptions on the facade over the portico are sacred verses written in gold. On the white ground on either side of the entrance, tile panels have been placed decorated with purple, red, green, and blue flowers and branches. These panels are some of the lovelist examples of 16th century tile-making. The leftmost of them is actually a copy of the one that was originally here and is now in the Louvre. The cornice sorrounding the entrance and the side decorations are done in exquisite floral tiles with a turquoise ground.

The lighting of the interior of the tomb has been very well arranged and the windows vary according to the walls. Between the windows, cabinets with carved doors have been placed. In order to provide lighting between the two floors, windows were also placed in the dome. Above the lower row of windows is one and a half meter-wide band of inscribed verses done in the *sülüs* style in white on a dark blue ground. Inside the tomb are forty-two sarcophagi of varying dimensions, the foot ends of which all point towards the door. Ahead of them all closest to the wall facing the entrance lies Sultan Selim II, who occupied the Ottoman throne for eight years, two months, and nineteen days. The sarcophagus is set on a marble-edged base. At the head and foot of the grave are large bronze candlesticks. To the sovereign's right lies his favourite wife, Nurbanu Valide Sultan, who was the mother of his son (later Murad III) and who died in 1585.

*The interior of the dome of Selim II's Mausoleum.*

# FOUNTAIN OF AHMED III

Elegant in its proportions, this square fountain was built in 1728. Five small domes top the broad-eaved roof. It has a glazed tile facing and niches with fountains at each of the four corners covered with gilded grills where water was once freely distributed to passersby. The light airy forms, the delicate color harmony of the decoration, and the charm of its volumes make this fountain one of the loveliest in Istanbul.

*Soğukçeşme street row houses, restored from ruins.*

*The fountain of Sultan Ahmed III.*

# HAGIA EIRENE

Located in the first courtyard of Topkapi Palace, this is the second largest church in the city after Hagia Sophia. It was dedicated to Divine Peace. These two churches with their monasteries, rest-homes for the elderly and other units, constituted the main religious centres in Byzantium. For a long time, Hagia Eirene housed the Patriarchate. The original building was destroyed by fire during the Nika Revolt along with Hagia Sophia (532). The second basilica was built double-domed in the 6th century by Justinian, and after extensive restorations has survived up to now. Hagia Eirene was not converted into a mosque. It was used as a military depot and a museum. After extensive restorations in recent years, it has been converted into a concert hall. It has unique acoustics, and every year in June many performances take place there during the traditional Istanbul Arts Festival. During the rest of the year it serves as a museum. Although it was built as a basilica, with its double domes and centrally located nave it looks different. Its low dome is original and it looks primitive. It is said that the original dome of Hagia Sophia was very similar to this one. The main dome acquired its shape in the 8th century following restorations. The Church of Hagia Eirene is the only church that has survived with its original atrium. In the 19th century when it was a museum, many porphyry sarcophagi were brought here, and today they are seen in the courtyard, a section of which was repaired during the Turkish era.

*Exterior view of the Church of Hagia Eirene.*

*A concert in Hagia Eirene during Istanbul Festival.*

The Palace of Topkapı, or Topkapı Saray, is an extraordinary complex of buildings spread out over one of the seven hills of Istanbul, in a splendid site above the Sea of Marmara and the Golden Horn. Constantine's imperial palace once stood here until it was abandoned and fell into ruin with the fall of the Empire.

When the Turks conquered Istanbul Mohammed II first chose the site of the present University as the seat for his palace, but later decided to rebuild the palace of Topkapi, which means «gate of the cannon». Begun in 1462, its principal parts were finished in 1478 and it was the official seat of the Ottoman sultans up until 1855 when Abdülmecid moved to the new and sumptuous palace of Dolmabahçe, built on the model of the ostentatious imperial residences of the west.

# ORTAKAPI

This is the central entrance gate to the palace, known also as Bâb-ı-Salaam, or «gate of salvation». Built in 1525 under Süleyman the Magnificent, it is flanked by two octagonal towers where those condemned to death were kept prisoner.

Only the sultan could pass through Bâb-ı-Salaam on horseback – all the others had to go on foot.

*Ceremony in the courtyard of the Topkapı Palace. A 16th century miniature.*

*Following pages: Ceremony in the presence of Sultan Selim III by the Gate of Felicity or of the White Eunuchs.*

*The Gate of Salvation.*

# TOPKAPI

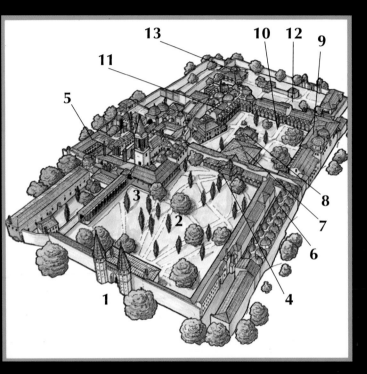

1 - Gate of Salvation
2 - Second courtyard
3 - Entrance to the Harem
4 - Gate of Felicity or of the White Eunuchs
5 - Harem
6 - Kitchens
(now housing the Porcelains section)
7- Audience Hall
8 - Library of Ahmed III
9 - Treasury
10 -Third courtyard
11- Room of the Relics
12 - Fourth courtyard
13 - Baghdad Pavilion

The kitchens of the palace.

Examples of Chinese porcelains (Ming Dynasty).

# KITCHENS
# (PORCELAINS SECTION)

On the right side of the second court one can see the palace kitchens with their twenty tall chimneys. In the days when the palace was living, more than 1000 assistant cooks worked in the kitchens, preparing the menus for the different parts of the palace. A part of the kitchens has been kept in its original state, and the rest has been converted into a museum where porcelains and china are exhibited. About 2500 of the 12000-plus pieces of chinaware of Chinese and Japanese origin in the palace collection is on display here. Furthermore, selected pieces of porcelains and glassware made in Istanbul are exhibited in chronological order. Recently this section of the Topkapi Palace Museum has been rearranged to include also European porcelains and silverware from the palace collection.

# THE THIRD COURTYARD AND THE GATE OF FELICITY

The entrance to the third court of the Topkapi Palace, the private court of the Sultans, is through the gate called Bab-i-Saadet (Gate of Felicity). Nobody without special permission could pass through that gate, and those with permission were admitted, only in the company of white eunuchs, to the Sultan's private court. Surrounding this court were the Palace University, the throne chamber, the Sultan's treasury and the sanctuary of Holy Islamic relics. The Sultan met with the ambassadors of foreign countries and the high officials of his government in the throne chamber that is located directly opposite the gate. The servants to the throne chamber were specially picked from deaf-mutes for obvious security reasons.

*The Library of Ahmed III.*

*The Gate of Felicity.*

# LIBRARY OF AHMED III

Located at the center of the courtyard this exquisite example of Turkish civil architecture, was built in 1719 during the age of tulips. The building is in white marble with a portico and with a central dome surrounded by smaller domes. The interior preserves a splendid wall decoration in faience from Iznik and is still used as a library with an important collection of antique and valuable manuscripts.

*The interior of the Library of Ahmed III.*

*Library of Ahmed III. Manuscript depicting Süleyman the Magnificent receiving the Prince of Transylvania.*

*Library of Ahmed III. Portrait of Selim II by Nigari, 1570 ca.*

*Library of Ahmed III. Manuscript depicting Süleyman the Magnificent's military campaigns in Europe.*

# THE TREASURY

The Treasury section of the Topkapi Palace Museum is the richest collection of its kind in the world. All the pieces exhibited in the four halls are authentic originals. Masterpieces of Turkish craftsmen from different centuries and priceless creations from the Far East, India and Europe fascinate the visitors. In each of the four rooms there is an imperial throne used in a different period of the empire. Ceremonial attire and accessories, weapons, water pipes, Turkish coffee cups and other vessels adorned with gold and precious stones are the main items in the first room. The second room is known as the "emeralds and other precious stones". Huge uncut emeralds weighing a few kilograms each and the Topkapi dagger with four large emeralds on the hilt and embellished with diamonds that has become the symbol of the palace is seen in this room. In the third room, enamelled pieces, medals and decora-

*A ceremonial canteen (16th century).*

*A jeweled jug (16th century).*

*A ceremonial canteen (16th century).*

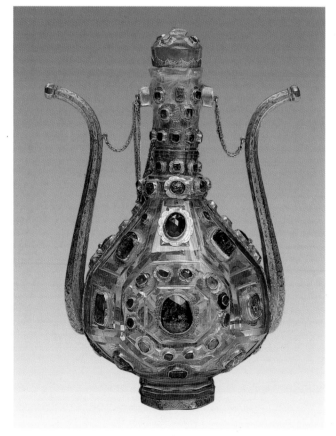

*Ceremonial throne.*

tions given to the Sultans by foreign countries, the twin solid gold candelabra each weighing 48 kilograms, and the most renowned throne in the palace – the golden throne used on the coronation day of the Sultans – are displayed. Connecting the third and fourth rooms is a balcony which commands a magnificient view of the entrance of the Bosphorus and the Asiatic coast. In the fourth room are the grand throne of Turko-Indian origin and many pieces adorned with precious stones which fascinate every visitor. In addition to the four rooms, there is also a very rich collection of watches, and table and wall clocks in a room across the treasury in the third courtyard.
The Holy Relics of Islam, which used to belong to the Prophet Mohammed are kept and exhibited in a special sanctuary by the third courtyard, and in an adjoining hall a collection illustrating the consummate skill of Turkish calligraphers is exhibited.

**Ceremonial throne** – The throne that the Turkish sultans used during the solemn investiture ceremonies is 178 cm. high and is in walnut completely sheathed with golden plaques for which 80,000 golden ducats where melted down.
It weighs 250 kilograms and 954 chrysolites are embedded in it. In 1585 it was presented to Murat III by the governor of Egypt Ibrahim Paşa and remained in the Topkapı palace even after the sultans had moved to the palace of Dolmabahçe.

*Throne of Nadir.*

*The splendid dagger and the "spoon" diamond.*

**Throne of Nadir** – Known also as the throne of Shah Ismail (it is thought to have belonged to him), it is basically an oval armchair on four legs 46 cm. high, made of ebony covered with gold, and with emeralds, rubies and pearls set into a layer of enamel. Along the outer border of the throne there are nine pine cones of rubies crowned by an emerald. The pillow, in purple velvet, is decorated with plaques of gold with flowers in pearls, rubies and turquoises. A costly work of Indian craftsmanship, it was brought back as war booty by Nadir Shah and presented to Sultan Mahmud I as a gift in 1746. Since it comes from India some scholars have even advanced the fascinating hypothesis that this precious throne belonged to no less a person than Tamerlane.

**Dagger** – This splendid jewel, so famous that it was even the protagonist of a celebrated film, was one of the gifts that Sultan Mahmud I sent to Nadir Shah in 1746. When the Turkish delegation arrived in Baghdad, they had news of a bloody revolution in Persia in which the shah himself had been killed. The Turkish ambassadors returned to Istanbul, taking all their gifts with them, including the dagger. It is 35 cm. long and encrusted with diamonds and with enamel decoration representing bowls of fruit on both sides. The hilt consists of three enormous emeralds surrounded by diamonds. Another octagonal cut emerald, which closes on a small watch, is at the tip of the hilt.

**The «spoon» diamond** – A jewel from *A Thousand and One Nights*, this diamond of 86 karats is surrounded by forty-nine extremely pure cut diamonds. There are two contrasting versions as to the stone's origin. The first, perhaps a legend, says that it was found in a refuse heap by a poor fisherman who sold it to a crafty jeweler in the bazaar in exchange for three spoons. This explains the name of the diamond, «kaşikçi», which in Turkish means «maker of spoons», although the jewel also recalls a spoon in its form. According to the second version which is certainly much more reliable, a French officer named Pigot bought it in 1774 from the Maharajah of Madras and took it to France. It changed hands several times and was put on auction, in which Giacomo Casanova is also said to have taken part, and was acquired by Napoleon's mother who however had to sell it in an attempt to save her son from exile. Then, for 150,000 gold coins it came into the possession of the governor Tepedelenli Alì Paşa who put it with the other jewels in his personal treasury.

When the governor was accused of treason and dismissed by Mahmud II, the diamond became part of the Ottoman treasury. It also seems likely that this diamond is the Pikot diamond, all track of which has been lost and which was also said to have been 86 karats.

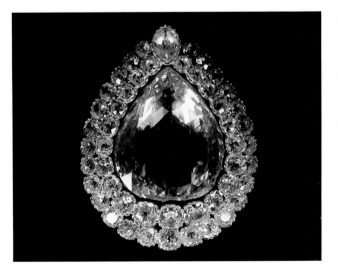

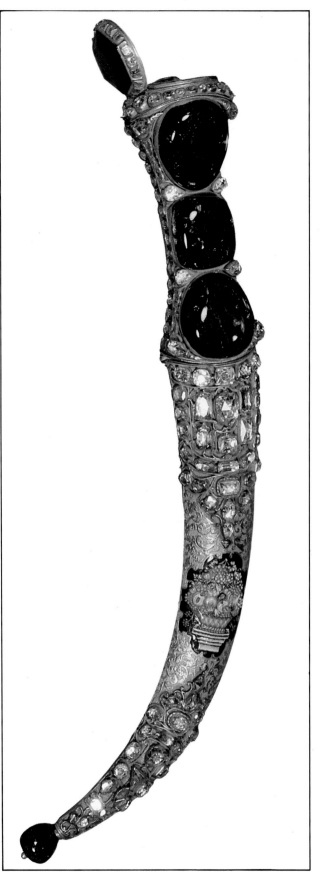

**Statuette of an elephant with a music box** – From India, where it was made in the early 18th century and given to the Ottoman court, it consists of a box decorated with landscapes which change when the music box is set in motion. The elephant on top is in silver covered with gold and the trappings are enriched with diamonds, rubies and emeralds.

**«The narghile smoker»** – This too comes from India and was given as a present to the sultan Abdülaziz. The statuette, a fine 19th century piece of work, consists of a single pearl of unusual size which forms the body and head of the Indian who is smoking the narghile. The turban is decorated with diamonds and rubies, while the cushion and the canopy and the basket of flowers in front of the man are precious elegant inlays of enamel with rubies and emeralds.

# BAGHDAD PAVILION

Erected in 1639 to perpetuate the memory of the conquest of the city of Baghdad by Murat IV, it is an elegant arcaded building, simple and harmoniously proportioned. The interior, completely sheathed in glazed tile from Iznik with floral motifs in turquoise, blue and white, is a single room on which four iwan open off. The decoration moves from these tiles, including the frieze with inscriptions from the Koran which runs all along the wall, to the doors which are finely inlaid in mother-of-pearl, ivory and tortoise shell.

To one side of the Baghdad Pavilion is *Ibrahim's baldachin* of 1640, a small dome in gilded copper on four slim columns. Sheltered here, Sultan Ibrahim partook of the meal which interrupted the ritual fast of Ramadan.

*This page, top: statuette with an elephant; bottom: "the narghile smokers".*

*Following page, top: the Baghdad Pavilion with Ibrahim's baldachin on the left; bottom: the interior of the Baghdad Pavilion.*

52

# THE IMPERIAL COSTUMES SECTION

There is no exhibition in the world than can compare to the Imperial Costumes Section of the Topkapi Palace Museum. The costumes made of fabric woven on the palace looms and ornamented with gold and silver braids have been carefully preserved since the 15th century and are in excess of 2,500 in number. Also exhibited in the same section are silk prayer rugs, masterpieces of Turkish art, that were used by the Sultans.

*Portrait of Selim III.*

*A jeweled ceremonial helmet.*

*Examples of caftans on display in the Imperial Costumes Section.*

A showcase in the center of the room contains the Prophet's bamboo bow and the swords of the first three caliphs.

The imprint in bronze of the Prophet's foot.

# ROOM OF THE RELICS

This room, sacred to the Islamic faith because it contains the relics of the prophet Mohammed, was built between 1464 and 1478 on the orders of Mohammed the Conqueror. Originally it was called the Imperial Chamber and it was here that the Sultan took care of the ordinary affairs of state. In the second decade of the 16th century, after Selim I's victorious campaign in Egypt, objects and relics sacred to the Muslim religion began to arrive in Istanbul. The most precious is without doubt the mantle that belonged to the Prophet and which is kept in the golden box incised with verses from the Koran which Sultan Aziz had made. The entire room is sheathed in fine old 16th century faience. In one corner, a large baldachin in gilded silver made by Derviş Zilli Mohammed, chief goldsmith of the palace at the time of Murat IV and father of Evliya Celebi, a great traveller who lived between 1611 and 1681. Other important relics are preserved in

this sacred spot: the bronze imprint of the Prophet's foot, his banner, his bow, and above his two swords: one with the scabbard and hilt in pure gold with precious stones, the other in iron with applications of gold on the upper part of the blade.

*The golden box which contains Mohammed's mantle and, in the foreground, his two swords. An ancient manuscript of the Koran is among the most precious relics kept here.*

# HAREM

The word harem derives from the Arab «harim» which means something forbidden and «haram», literally sanctuary. The harem was in fact the private residence of the sultan, the quarter where the women in the palace lived – the Turkish sovereign's mother, his sister, his wives, his concubines. Our information on the harem in Istanbul goes back as far as 1578. The harem occupies a large space inside Topkapı and today covers an area of circa 15,000 square meters. The vast architectural complex consists of various buildings in different forms and styles, for the sultans kept on modifying the ensemble, adding buildings with no regard for an organic plan, and tying them together by means of courtyards and corridors, until a real labyrinth came to be formed. The harem was governed by a corps of black eunuchs, almost all Abyssinians who had been offered to the Sultan by the pasha of Egypt when they were young. Their task was to guard the entrances to the harem so that no outsider might enter the apartments reserved to the women.

**Twin pavilions** – Known also as the «Apartments of the heir» they are two communicating rooms facing on the courtyard of the favorites and the pool of the concubines. The 17th century ceramics on the walls represent tulips, roses, hyacinths, cypresses. The same floral motifs are in the glazed panels in the windows. Next to the chimney are two fine panels with intarsias of ebony and mother-of-pearl.

**Room of Murat III** – This is one of the loveliest rooms in the harem. The perfect proportions of the elegant dome reveal the touch of the great Sinan who seems to have built this room in 1578. Embellished with a fireplace with a copper hood and various niches in which to keep the objects of daily use, the room also has a monumental fountain, supposedly because the sound of the running water covered the voices of the people who were inside the room.

**Library of Ahmed I** – The room of Murat III leads to the small delightful reading room of Ahmed I. The niches were probably meant to hold the books of the sultan who was a great lover of literature and a poet. On the wall are horizontal inscriptions of verses from the Koran. On the vertical borders around the windows there are poetic texts which some say were written by the sultan himself.

**Imperial Hall** – This is the largest room in the harem, begun under Süleyman the Magnificent by Sinan but radically changed in 1750 with the insertion of mirrors which conceal secret doors, of wainscotting, and marble columns. The decoration on the wall was also changed and the faience from the workshops of Iznik was replaced by the blue and white tiles of Delft. Here, the sultan and the women of the harem participated in parties, balls and entertainment.

**Ahmed III's Fruit Room** – Palace chronicles say that Sultan Ahmed III had little appetite and in the hopes of getting him to eat a bit, this room was decorated with lacquered wood panels on which are painted exotic fruits (alternated with bouquets of flowers) enclosed in geometric frames. Created in the early 18th century, this is one of the most unusual rooms in the entire palace.

# BURNT COLUMN

One of the first monuments in the city (it dates to 325 A. D.), it was built by Constantine I. Originally 57 meters high, today all that is left is a corroded truncated column not much more than 34 meters high. Once a statue of Constantine I as the god Apollo stood on the top. In 1105 the bronze statue toppled and was replaced by a capital and a golden cross. It is said that the emperor had had the symbols of pagan and Christian tradition walled up in the marble pedestal of the column, including an image of Athena from Troy, the stone from which Moses had brought forth water, bread which was left over after Christ had fed the multitudes. The same tradition says that in the crown which decorated the statue of Constantine-Apollo the nails from Christ's cross had been fused.

# JUSTINIAN'S CISTERN

The Yerebatan Sarayi, or submerged castle, is an enormous and impressive subterranean cistern which Justinian had built between 527 and 565 to provide water for the surrounding houses in case of war. It is 141 meters long and 73 meters wide with a vault supported by twelve rows of columns 8 meters high whose bases are submerged in water. The 336 columns have Corinthian capitals.

*Preceding page: the burnt Column and two views of the Justinian's cistern.*

*Entrance to the Museums.*

# ISTANBUL ARCHAEOLOGICAL MUSEUMS

Istanbul Archaeological Museum is a complex of three museums: the Museum of Oriental Antiquities, the Archaeological Museum and the Tiled Pavilion Museum. The complex is located in the gardens in the first court of the Topkapı Palace. There are sixty-thousand archaeological treasures, seven-hundred-sixty thousand coins and medallions, and seventy-five thousand clay tablets in these three museum.

The Archaeological Museum was founded by the famous painter, archaeologist and curator of the time, Osman Hamdi, and opened to the public of June 13, 1891 under the name Müze-i Hümayun (the Imperial Museum). The museum, which was re-arranged and enlarged by the addition of a new wing to the building, was reopened to the public on its centennial. The gate of this majestic building de-

signed by architect Valaury is monumental.

In the halls to the right of the entrance, examples of "Antique Age Sculpture" are exhibited. Unique examples of sculpture from the Archaic age until the end of Roman era are exhibited in the halls of "Antique Crave Stones and Reliefs", "Treasures from Persian Reign in Anatolia", Kenan Erim Hall (Aphrodisias Relics), "Three Marble Cities in Anatolia" (Ephesus, Miletus, Aphrodisias), "Hellenistic Sculpture", "Magnesia AD meandrum and Tralles (Aydin) Statue Groups" "Hellenistic and Hellenistic Influenced Roman Sculpture", "Roman Art of Portrait Making", "Roman Empire Sculpture". The majority of these artifacts was discovered during the excavations of the ancient cities in Anatolia. Following the counters, where sou-

*Relief of a bull. Brickwork from the Ishtar Gate, Babylon (604-562 B.C.)*

*The statue of Marsyas.*

venirs and book are sold, on the left of the entrance, is the hall dedicated to Osman Hamdi, the founder of the museum. Right after this hall, treasures unearthed during the excavation of the Royal Cemetery in Sidon are exhibited. Excavation of the Cemetery was carried on by Osman Hamdi, himself. The first of the three sarcophagi standing side by side belongs to Tabnit, the king of Sidon. A unique Lician sarcophagus and a Satrap sarcophagus are also found in this hall. Next comes the world famous Sarcophagus of Alexander the Great and the Sarcophagus of the Mourning Women. Both these sarcophagi were discovered during the excavation of the Royal Cemetery in Sidon and they date back to the 4th century B.C. Various architectural frag-

ments are displayed in the annex building. In its ground level is the hall of "Antique Age Anatolian Architecture" and in the first storey is the hall of "Istanbul Through the Centuries". On the second storey, small archaeological finds belonging to the Paleolithic age, Early, Middle and Late Bronze ages and the Frigian State age in Anatolia are displayed under the heading "Anatolia Through the Centuries and Troy". A section of this hall is reserved for the artifacts found in Troy and the treasures discovered in the settlements I-IX are displayed in separate showcases. On the third storey, under the heading of "Civilisations in Anatolia and Its Vicinity", treasures discovered in Cyprus, Palestine and Syria are displayed in chronological order.

*Battle scene on the Alexander's sarcophagus. Pentelic marble, end of the 4th century B.C.*

*Sarcophagus of the Mourning Women. Pentelic marble, 4th century B.C.*

*Terracotta vase and glass from Troy.*

**Alexander's Sarcophagus** – Executed at the end of the 4th cent. B. C., the name refers to the battle scene represented and not to the fact that it may or may not have belonged to the great Macedonian soldier. The sarcophagus was found in 1887 by the director of the museum, Osman Hamdi Bey, during the excavations at Sido. It is in pentelic marble, 3.18 meters long and 2.12 meters high, and still preserves traces of the original paint. On its long sides are represented crowded battle scenes between Greeks and Persians, narrated with a serrated rhythm. On the end, are hunting scenes with lions, deer and a panther, containing fewer figures and with a greater feeling for air and space. The sarcophagus probably was meant for the mortal remains of a Phoenician prince.

*Marble statues of Artemis and Cleopatra, 2nd century A.D.*

*Apollo playing the lyra, marble statue, 2nd century A.D.*

*Oceanus (god of the rivers), marble statue from Ephesus, 2nd century A.D.*

# MUSEUM OF ORIENTAL ANTIQUITIES

The building housing the museum was constructed in 1883 to house the Academy of Fine Arts. In 1974, it was turned into a museum to exhibit the treasures of Egyptian, Mesopotamian, Arab and early Anatolian civilizations. Archives of Clay Tablets bearing cuneiform script occupies the ground floor. With its approximately seventy-five thousand pieces, the collection ranks second in the world after the British Museum.

# THE TILED PAVILION

It is the first pavilion built in the Topkapi Palace complex by Mehmet the Conqueror, in 1492. Its facade, decorated with columns and arches, and the decorations of its antechamber and tiled walls are typical examples of Seljouk influenced early Ottoman architecture. The antechamber is decorated with a long inscription created by multicolored, cut tiles. 12th to 19th century Seljouk and Ottoman tiles and ceramics are displayed in the rooms in chronological order. 16th century Iznik tiles are also on exhibit in the museum

*View of the interior of the Museum of Oriental Antiquities.*

*The tiled pavilion.*

# THE COVERED BAZAR

The oldest and the largest covered market place in the world is situated in the centre of the city. Resembling a giant labyrinth, it consists of approximately sixty lanes and more than three thousand shops. This unique and interesting market place is one of those places in the city which one must see to really appreciate.

The city-like bazaar is completely covered and it has grown in size over the centuries. At its centre is a thick walled 15th century original structure covered by a series of domes. The new streets that formed on both sides of the structure were also covered, thus enlarging the shopping area. In the old days, each street was reserved for a different profession and the quality of the handicrafts, produced here was strictly controlled. Business practices were governed by strict traditional ethics. Every kind of valuable fabric, jewellery, weapons and antique objects used to be sold by merchants from families which, for generations, had dealt in the same trade. They were experts in their fields.

The bazaar survived earthquakes and a few fires towards the end of the last century. During the restorations, it lost its original form and features, and has changed for the worse. In the old days, people used to trust the merchants here and lend them money; as they deposit money in the banks today.

Today, many of the streets in the bazaar have changed character. Guilds such as the "quilt makers", "slipper makers" and "fez makers" exist only in the street names.

Jewellers line the main street in the bazaar. The goldsmiths are on a side street at right angles to the main street. Prices vary, and bargaining is customary in these rather small stores.

## SHOPPING IN ISTANBUL

The Grand Bazaar of Istanbul with its thousands of shops is a famous and unique shopping centre. BAZAAR 54, the leading establishment in the Grand Bazaar, offers fully washed, top quality handmade carpets selected by experts. The old and new carpet collection of BAZAAR 54, containing thousands of items of top quality Turkish workmanship, are Istanbul's largest and richest.

BAZAAR 54 is an authorized exporter with worldwide shipping service. Next to carpets, its handmade, fully guaranteed jewellery collection is also worth seeing. Outstanding samples of Turkish souvenirs as well as quality leather and suede apparel at bargain prices are also offered in Bazaar 54.

Traditional Turkish handmade jewellery has a well-deserved reputation of satisfying both modern and old-fashioned tastes.

*A few aspects of the covered bazar.*

The University of Istanbul in Bayazid square.

# THE UNIVERSITY

It is the first university founded in Istanbul and the original building today houses the office of administration of the university. Sultan Mehmet the Conqueror built the first Ottoman palace on the ground of this campus. After the construction of the Tokpapı Palace, the first Ottoman palace was referred to as the old palace. The building standing today was erected between 1864 and 1865 by the architect Bourgois to house the Ministry of Defense. When the Government offices were relocated to Ankara after the foundation of the Turkish Republic, the Ottoman University was moved here and in 1933 it was renamed the University of Istanbul. The three-storied building made of stone covers an area of 124X44 metres and it is sorrounded by a large garden. The Bayazid Yangin Kulesi (the fire lookout tower) is the other main building in the garden. The original tower was built of wood in 1749. In 1828, upon the order of Sultan Mahmut II, it was rebuilt of stone. The tower, built in the Ottoman baroque style stands 85 metres tall. The monumental gate facing the Bayazid Square was also built by Bourgois in 1865.

# MOSQUE OF BAYAZID II

Also known as the «mosque of the doves» (a legend narrates that Bayazid II bought a pair of doves from a poor widow and gave them to the mosque), it was built between 1501 and 1506 by the architect Haydreddin and represents an important link between the 15th century Anatolian mosques and those built by Sinan.

There are similarities with Hagia Sophia, with a central dome supported on four pillars and two smaller side aisles, with granite and jasper columns which support pointed arches.
Inside there are numerous inscriptions by Seyd Hamdullah, the greatest calligrapher in the Islamic world.

*The Mosque of Bayazid II seen from Bayazid square.*

# SEHZADE MOSQUE

This lovely mosque was a youthful work of Sinan who finished it in 1548. A sad tale lies at the origin of the mosque. Süleyman the Magnificent had designated his first-born son Mustafa as successor to the throne but his favorite Roxelane was jealous and started to spread false rumors and plot against the young prince until finally Süleyman himself ordered his son to be killed. Mohammed's brother Cihangir went mad with grief. Repenting what he had done and to make amends for his guilt in causing the death of the two youths, innocent victims of Roxelane's jealousy, Süleyman had the Mosque of Sehzade built. The two brothers were buried together in a mausoleum in the garden.

*The interior of the dome.*

*The Sehzade Mosque.*

# MOSQUE OF SULTAN SÜLEYMAN

«I have built for thee, O Emperor, a mosque that will remain on the face of the earth until the day of judgement». This is what Sinan is said to have exclaimed when he completed the imposing structure of the mosque. And it is also said that after he had laid the foundations of the building Sinan disappeared until they consolidated – and that three whole years passed before he was absolutely certain of their stability. In any case the Süleymaniye is conclusive proof of the genius of this great Turkish architect, the «father» of Ottoman architecture, who was almost a contemporary of Michelangelo. With reference to this mosque Sinan said that it was only the work of a good craftsman as he considered himself to be. Built between 1550 and 1557, it has four slender minarets on the outside, a symbol that

Süleyman was the fourth Ottoman sultan, while the ten galleries which run along the minarets refer to the fact that he was the tenth sultan of the reigning dynasty. The interior is truly overwhelming in the grandeur of its proportions, the austerity of its aspect, the absence of any excessive ornamentation. Almost square, it is dominated by an enormous dome on a drum, 53 meters high. One hundred and thirty-eight windows flood the hall with variegated light. The only decorative elements are the lovely inscriptions by Ahmed Karahisari, one of the greatest 16th-century Turkish calligraphers, and the elegant white-ground ceramic tiles with flowers and leaves in turquoise, blue, and red, from the kilns in Iznik, ancient Nicaea, famous not only for the two councils held there but also for its ceramic art.

*The Süleyman Mosque and its complex.*

*Following pages: three views of the inner courtyard of the Süleyman Mosque.*

*Aquaduct of Valens.*

Three views of the interior of the Süleyman Mosque.

Portrait of Roxelane, favorite wife of Süleyman the Magnificent.

# TURBEH OF SÜLEYMAN THE MAGNIFICENT

Behind the mosque, in a small cemetery is the turbeh of Süleyman, which may also be by Sinan. Octagonal in form, the dome is supported by eight slender porphyry columns. Here the great sultan, who died in 1566 at the age of 71, reposes on an imposing catafalque, next to his daughter Mihrimah and the other two sovereigns, Süleyman II and Ahmed II. Nearby, another mausoleum, also octagonal in shape, belongs to Roxelane, literally the Russian, because that is where she was supposedly from. She was the great Süleyman's favorite: for her he repudiated all the other women in his harem and gave her the name of Hürrem, the «laughing one».

*Two aspects of the turbeh (mausoleum) of Süleyman the Magnificent.*

*One of the windows of the mausoleum.*

*The interior of the mausoleum.*

# YENI CAMI

The last of the great mosques built during the golden period of the Ottoman empire, it was begun in 1597 and finished in 1663. Its proportions are particularly harmonious and its courtyard is surrounded by a portico decorated in blue faience and covered with 25 domes. At the center is a delicate octagonal fountain.

*The Yeni Cami or New Mosque seen from the Galata Bridge.*

*The pulpit and the prayer niche inside the Yeni Cami.*

# EGYPTIAN MARKET

This long building covered by a row of low domes is where foodstuffs, above all spices, are sold in a fascinating oriental atmosphere where the air is redolent with its wares. The market was built in 1660 by the Sultana Turhan Hatiçe, mother of Mohammed IV, at a time when most drugs, colors and spices came from Egypt, on the site of a precedent covered market used by the Venetians.

*Two views of the Egyptian Market.*

A view of the flowers market.

A Turkish fast-food "Döner".

Water-pipe smokers.

A view of the interior of the Turkish Baths.

Fried fish sandwich sellers at Eminönü. A typical view of Istanbul.

Flower sellers at Taksim.

A Turkish bride.

Broom-sellers market at Bayazid.

# MOSQUE OF MOHAMMED II

Mohammed II the Conqueror ordered the construction of the mosque in the second half of the 15th century, on the ruins of the church of the Twelve Apostles. Destroyed in 1766 eartquake, the mosque was rebuilt in Baroque style by architect Tahir Ağa in 1771. The entrance portico and the inner courtyard remain of the original building. In the interior, the pulpit and the prayer niche are worth of note.

# TURBEH OF MOHAMMED II

In the garden of the mosque, to the southeast of the vast ensemble, is the turbeh of Mohammed II and his wife Gülbahar, built in 1782. An elaborate sarcophagus covered with an embroidered drape and surmounted by an enormous turban set in the direction of Mecca contains the remains of the Sultan.

*Details of the decorations in the ceiling of the Mosque (above) and of the Mausoleum (below).*

*The elaborate sarcophagus which contains the mortal remains of Mohammed the Conqueror, who died in 1481.*

The Genealogy of Christ, in the southern dome of the narthex.

Kariye Camii, the ancient church of the St.Saviour in Chora.

# ST. SAVIOUR IN CHORA (Kariye Camii)

Today the ancient church of the Saviour in Chora is the utmost example of the high level of achievement of Byzantine art. Despite the destruction of the iconoclastic period the mosaics and frescoes of the church are still practically perfect, as fresh and intact in their style and values as the day they were made.

The original building was the monastery of the Saviour in Chora (a mosaic in the outer narthex bears the inscription «chora ton zondon» where chora means country) and it was outside the city until the emperor Theodosius II included it in his new city walls. Restored, enlarged and embellished by the treasurer of Andronicus II, the humanist Theodore Metochites (who was buried there when he died), it was a church until 1511 when the vizier

Hadim Ali Paşa added a minaret and transformed it into a mosque. The original sanctuary consisted of a single square nave with a narthex and a semicircular apse. Theodore Metochites had the outer narthex and the parakklesion (mortuary chapel) added and also commissioned the mosaic decoration and the frescoes which were executed between 1305 and 1320.

In the main church, near the entrance door, is the moving mosaic with the *Dormition of the Virgin,* who is shown lying on her deathbed surrounded by a crowd of disciples and faithful, each with a different expression of grief on his face. The scene is divided in half by the figure of Christ, wrapped in a divine nimbus, who holds the soul of Mary, represented as a swaddling babe, in His arms.

The Genealogy of Christ. Inner narthex, southern dome.

Virgin and Child, dome of the parakklesion.

Christ healing a multitude, detail.

The Birth of the Virgin.

ΗΓΕΝΝΗΣΙΣΤΗΣ ΘΚ

Mosaic panel depicting the Census, mosaic of the
outer narthex.

Theodore Metochites offers Christ a model of the church,
mosaic in the narthex.

16th century fresco in the apse of the parakklesion: the
Resurrection.

St. Cyril and St. Gregory of Alexandria, the Fathers of the
Church, fresco in the apse of the parakklesion.

In the dome to the right of the narthex at the center
of a medallion is the imposing figure of *Christ the
Pantocrator* with the Gospels grasped in His left
hand and His right raised in a gesture of blessing.
Twenty-four segments radiate from Him with repre-
sentations of His ancestors, from Adam to Japheth.
This same kind of subdivision into segments is to be
found in the fresco in the outer narthex, with the
representation of the *Virgin and Child,* who appear
to be surrounded by a mystical halo consisting of
twelve segments each of which ends in a window.
Above these is an angel armed with a spear with a
sacred inscription.

# THE GALATA BRIDGE

The first bridge over the Golden Horn which connects the new city with the old was built by the Byzantine Emperor Justinian. After this, eleven bridges were built during Byzantium Period.

The present Galata Bridge was first wooden and constructed by Sultan II, Mahmut in 1836. It was replaced with metal span one in 1870. The new Galata Bridge, completed in 1992, is the fifth to have spanned this reach of the Golden Horn since the wooden one. It is a technical improvement on the extant old bridge whose pantoons do much to prevent the movement of fresh water into the Golden Horn. Two drawbridges open to allow shipping to pass and social pedestrian walkway and restaurants of the old bridge are being retained on a new footpath. The bridge is 450 m. long and 42 m. width.

*Fish sellers at Eminönü.*

*The Bosphorus seen from Eminönü.*

*The Topkapi Palace seen from Eminönü.*

*The Galata Bridge.*

*The city walls.*

# THE CITY WALLS

The historic city of Istanbul is located on a triangular peninsula which is surrounded by city walls on three sides. The walls seen today were built during the Roman era and extend a total of 22 km.

After the establishment of Byzantum, the city was enlarged four times, and each time the city walls were built more towards the west.

Because of its geographical location, the peninsula is easily defendable. Not so rugged terrain extending from the Balkans end against the colossal city walls on the landward side of the city. There were sturdy city walls along the shores of the Golden Horn and the Sea of Marmara too.

Nothing has remained from the first walls built around the acropolis of Byzantium, the second walls built in the beginning of the 3rd century by Emperor Septimius Severus, and the third walls built in the 320s by Constantine the Great.

The most important city wall was the one in the west, on the landward side. This extraordinarily strong wall stretched from the sea to the Golden Horn and was built in three different periods. There are many inscriptions pertaining to the restoration of the city walls during the late Byzantine and Turkish eras. The original single-rowed, high city walls on the land side were built over a short period by Emperor Theodosius II in 414 against possible attacks by the Huns (a 5,543 metres section extending from the sea to Tekfur Sarayi or the Palace of the Sovereign).

A strong earthquake in 447 caused extensive damage to these walls. During the restorations, another row of walls and a trench were built in front of this main city wall (11 metres in height). Near the other

side of the trench, a wall with embrasures was also constructed to create a four-staged defence system. The main city walls were fortified by 96 towers at approximately 55 metre intervals. The lower walls had 92 towers.

The trench in front of the walls measured 5-7 metres deep and 15-20 metres wide. Although certain sources indicate that the trenches were filled with water, due to the uneven topography of the land and shortage of water in the city this is highly unlikely. During an attack, it is much easier to cross a trench filled with water, anyway.

The city walls of Istanbul are a splendid example of Roman military architecture. Rows of bricks followed by rows of stone were used to create a colourful appearance.

The walls of Theodosius extend as far as Tekfur Sarayi. The tall, single row of walls that start at Tekfur Sarayi, have towers built close to each other. These were completed in the 12th century during the reign of Manuel I Comnenus.

*The Tekfur Palace or Palace of the Sovereign.*

*Following page: the imposing Yedikule Fortress and a view of the Mihrimah Mosque.*

# TEKFUR PALACE

Roman and early Byzantine palaces used to be situated near the Hippodrome. The Blachernae Palace where the Byzantine emperors lived, probably from the 7th or 8th centuries until the conquest, was spread over a wide area where the city walls reached the Golden Horn. The only surviving pavilion of this palace complex is the Palace of the Tekfur and it was built adjacent to the city walls.

The three-storeyed pavilion (its roof is missing) was built in the 12th century. It has a small courtyard and its ornate facade is decorated with rows of bricks and stone. Its windows were given a dynamic appearance by rows of arches and supports. The ground floor opens onto the courtyard. The second storey of the pavilion has access to the Thedosius City Walls.

In the 18th century, the palace was used as a workshop to produce tiles.

# YEDIKULE

One of the finest views of the Sea of Marmara can be had from this spot where an imposing fortress in the shape of a regular star-shaped polygon with five defensive towers rose in Byzantine times. Later two more towers were added and since then the fortress has been known as «Castle of the Seven Towers» or Heptapyrgion in Greek and Yedikule in Turkish. A famous state prison, the eastern tower is known as the «tower of the inscriptions» from the numerous messages the unfortunate prisoners left incised on its walls.

# MIHRIMAH MOSQUE

On the Asian coast of Uskudar, the imposing Mihrimah Mosque rises where there was once a Byzantine church dedicated to St. George. It was erected in 1550 by the great Sinan in honor of Mihrimah, wife of the grand vizier Rustem Paşa and daughter of Süleyman the Magnificent and Roxelane.

# EYÜP MOSQUE

Not only is it considered the holy mosque of Istanbul but, after the Mecca and Jerusalem, it may even be the third holy place for pilgrims in the Islamic world. Its fame lies in the fact that this is the burial place of the standard bearer of the prophet Mohammed, Eyüp-ül-Ensârî-Halit Bin Zeyd, who was struck down and buried in the battle field during the first siege of Constantinople by the Arabs in 669. At the time of the great siege, in 1453 the story goes that Mohammed the Conqueror saw in a dream the place where Eyüp was buried. When he had the spot dug up he found what he had seen in his dream. The sultan then had a mosque built, which soon became the object of pilgrimages and a place of worship. Every time a sultan mounted the throne it was here that the ceremony of the conferral of the new sword was held and the newly elected sultan was girded with the sword of Osman, symbol of the caliphate. Gleaming white, the internal walls sheathed in ceramic tiles with red and yellow flowers on a blue ground, the mosque is enlivened by the flight of herons, storks and pigeons which have built their nests under the courtyard portico.

*View of the Eyüp Mosque.*

Behind the Eyüp Mosque, on top of the hill, is a small wooden building, typically oriental in its architecture and decoration. This is the café whose name pays homage to the famous French writer Pierre Loti (1850-1923), pseudonym of Louis Marie Julien Viaud, who came here to work and contemplate the lovely panorama. Today, despite the fact that the surroundings have lost much of their ancient beauty, the view is marvelous: from the tangle of streets and roofs beyond the glimmer of the Golden Horn, the pointed minarets of the mosques of Istanbul stand out against the sky. The interior of the café has been kept as it was when the author of the *Fishermen of Iceland* (whose books and portraits are still to be found inside) sat at these tables.

*A panoramic view of the Golden Horn, the historical Peninsula and the Galata district from the Café of Pierre Loti.*

*The interior of the Café of Pierre Loti furnished in the traditional Ottoman style.*

# GALATA TOWER

Many sources say that a tower stood here as early as the year 500, probably a light-house. It is however certain that one was erected by the Genovese in 1216. Damaged by numerous fires in various periods, it was restored by Selim II and used as a prison under Suleyman the Magnificent. Today, 45 meters high and crowned by a characteristic conical roof, it is a splendid place to get a panorama of the city.

*The Galata Tower.*

*The Turkish belly-dancers.*

*Taksim Square.*

# TÜNEL - BEYOĞLU and TAKSIM

Tünel (the subway) which connects the shores of the Golden Horn to the Beyoğlu district on the hill, is located in Karaköy Square. This second metro in Europe was opened for services in 1880 and today, it is the shortest line in the world.

**Istiklal Caddesi -** The street stretches on the hills in the Beyoğlu district, and starts at the upper entrance to "Tunel", and extends all the way to Taksim Square. Beginning in the 16th century, Beyoğlu became the district where foreign embassy buildings were constructed and minorities lived. Near the upper entrance to Tünel is the Galata Mevlevihanesi which is a museum today. The lodge is the most interesting of its kind. There are interesting collections of books and musical instruments in the Divan Edebiyatl (old Ottoman Poetry) Museum on the first floor of the lodge.

When Ankara became the capital after the foundation of the Turkish Republic, all the foreign embassies were moved to the new capital, and the old embassy buildings in Istanbul were converted into consulates.

Istiklal Caddesi used to be the main street famous for its elegant shops, lively and colourful nightlife, theatres and cinemas, but in recent years it has deteriorated. In 1990, to improve the area, the traffic was rerouted, a tramway line was installed all along the street and the buildings were renovated. The Catholic churches seen on the side of the street overlooking the Bosphorus have held services since the last century.

**Taksim Square -** Halfway towards the Taksim Square is the small Galatasaray Square where the famous lycée of the same name is located. Near the square, there is a partially collapsed building known as the Flower Passage, where there are many small restaurants and beerhouses. The street running next to this passage is lined with shops selling many varieties of fish, vegetables and fruit.

Taksim Square, surrounded by the Atatürk Cultural Centre in the north and five star hotels, is considered the centre of Istanbul and the Atatürk Monument is in the center of the square.

This is one of the leading museums of its kind in the world. It occupies two large buildings located in the gardens of the Officers' Club near the Hilton Hotel. In the two-storeyed main older section, military uniforms, weapons, and tools used in the Empire and the Republic are displayed. The new building is reserved for old tents including the imperial tents.

# THE JANISSARY BAND

The official band of the Ottoman army was known as the Mehter. This band of thousands of members used to lead the armies going on campaigns. The band, which had its own special way of marching, used to play stirring marches during attacks and sieges. Today, the oldest band in the world still lays its music in its own characteristic style, on certain days in the Military Museum, and during special ceremonies and concerts.

*The Janissary Band during a performance.*

*The Dolmabahçe Palace seen from the sea.*

# DOLMABAHÇE PALACE

About three centuries ago there was a broad bay whose waters sheltered many ships in the place now occupied by Dolmabahçe Palace. Under the sultanates of Ahmed I and Osman II the bay was filled in and it was then that it received its name of Dolma Bahçe which means «filled-in graden». In the beginning the palace was a simple wooden pavilion, which was enlarged as time went by, and here the sultans used to pass the hot summer months. After having been partly destroyed by fire more than once, it was radically transformed, for the old palace of Topkapı was too old fashioned and too small for the requirements of the numerous court of Sultan Mahmud II. His successor, Abdülmecid, followed his example and transferred definitively to Dolmabahçe, abandoning Topkapı Saray for ever. The present palace, designed by the architect Karabet Balian, was built in emulation of the sumptuous royal residences of the West in 1843 and later. Halfway between a moorish castle, a baroque Italian palazzo and a Hindu temple, the Dolmabahçe Palace was built with marble from the nearby islands in the sea of Marmara. Preceded by a sumptuous portal in «Turkish Renaissance» style, it covers an area that is 284 meters long. Finished in 1856, it is said that the cost was five million Turkish gold lira, more than a hundred million dollars at the current rate of exchange.

The interior is ostentatious, glittering with gold and marble, crystal, alabaster and porphyry. The long wings of the palace contain 285 rooms, 43 halls, six bath rooms. The floors of the halls are covered by 4,455 square meters of precious hand-woven carpets and chandeliers in Baccarat and Bohemian crystal hang from the ceilings. The most important of these is the one in the Great Hall, the «Muayade Salonu». It was given to the sultan by Queen Victoria and has 750 lights, weighs four and a half tons and is said to be the largest chandelier in the world. The room in which it is hung is also impressive in its size: it

*The Great Hall in the Dolmabahçe Palace.*

measures 40x45 meters, with a dome 36 meters high painted in *trompe l'oeil*. Every hall in the palace is decorated and furnished with luxuriant pomp: Chinese, Japanese and European porcelain, golden clocks, crystal and silver chandeliers, mirrors with elaborate frames.

*The room of the Ambassadors,* with a lovely ceiling of gilded stucco and rosettes, contains four fireplaces with crystal mirrors, Sèvres vases and Chinese porcelains. Historically the hall is also important, for outstanding decisions of state were made there in the last part of the Ottoman sultanate.

*The Pink Room,* so-called because the color pink predominates in the decoration, is the second most important hall in the harem. The bronze braziers

The Blue Room.

The Room of the Ambassadors.

*The interior decorations of the Dolmabahçe Palace exhibit the characteristics of Baroque, Rococo and Empire style. Ottoman style pen work decorations are also seen in certain places.*

*Next to the palace overlooking the sea is the lovely Dolmabahçe Mosque, which was begun in 1853 by Abdülmecid's mother. Formerly seat of the Admiralty, it is now a naval museum with a rich collection of figureheads, weapons and uniforms.*

which dominate the room were once used for heating, until the modern radiators, their upper parts gilded, were installed.

*The Blue Room,* which also derives its name from the dominating color, is particularly lovely. The induction ceremony of the sultans Abdülmecid II and Mohammed V took place there. Illuminated by three large windows set into both facades, the ceiling is decorated with large floral panels enclosed in elaborate gilded frames. A beautiful chandelier in red and white crystal hangs from the ceiling, below which is a marble table with gilded reliefs and a monumental French vase of 1869. There are also many Chinese and Japanese vases along the sides of the hall.

On November 10, 1938, Kemal Atatürk died in a small room in this sumptuous palace. He had al-ready transferred the capital to Ankara, in the heart of the country, and had turned this palace into an important center for international congresses. Upon entering the palace the visitor in struck by the fact that all the clocks have stopped at 9:05 a.m. This was the hour in which the great statesman, the father of modern Turkey, closed his eyes for ever. It is a small homage to the great man who had dedicated his entire life to the birth and growth of his country. Throughout the years many famous people visited and stayed here: from the French Empress Eugénie to the Austrian Emperor Francis Joseph; from the German Emperor William II to King Peter of Serbia, and, more recently, Reza Pahlavi Shah of Iran, Edward Prince of Wales and the French President Charles de Gaulle.

*The Ortaköy Mosque.*

*A view of the Bebek.*

# BEBEK

An image of the old wooden houses of Istanbul which still exist in the Bebek quarter, one of the most elegant and aristocratic in the city. In olden times it was called Challae and was the site of a temple dedicated to Diana, goddess of the chase.

Later Selim I built a palace here and in 1725 Sultan Ahmed III built another one.
No trace of these is left today and elegant modern buildings rise where they used to be.

*Three views of the Rumeli Hisari, the imposing European Fortress.*

# RUMELI HISARI, THE EUROPEAN FORTRESS

The city had been beseiged many times before the final seige by the Conqueror in 1453, but had managed to defend itself with the help of the Roman city walls. Even during long seiges, provisions were brought into the city from sea. Therefore, to prevent any reinforcements and help coming from the Black Sea during the seige, before the final seige started, a fortress was built on the European shore, opposite the other Turkish fortress built earlier on the Asian shore. The fortress was completed in an amazingly short time of four months in 1452. This largest and strongest fortress of the Middle Ages was no more important right after the fall of the city. A fine ex-

ample of classic Turkish fortress architecture, this impressive fortress is another element adorning the Bosphorus. It was restored in the 1950s and turned into a museum. During the annual Festival of Arts, gardens of the fortress is used as an amphitheatre.
It is viewed best from the Asian shores or from the boats operating on the Bosphorus.
The campus of Boğaziçi (Bosphorus) University is spread on the slopes behind the fortress. Robert College, the first American educational institution established outside the United States, used to occupy this campus. In 1967, the college was turned into a university.

*Preceding pages: a view of the Ortaköy district and the Bosphorus bridge at night.*

# THE BOSPHORUS

One of the most beautiful sights in the world, the Bosphorus, is a strait that runs a winding course between the two continents from one sea to another. It is a natural border between Europe and Asia and it is the only outlet of the Black Sea which is connected to the Aedean through the Bospohorus and the Dardanelles. With old seaside mansions, mosques, palaces, restaurants and beaches along its shores, the Bosphorus resembles a wide river. Woods and residences cover the hills rising behind its shores. The Bosphorus is unforgettable. Two fortresses, constructed halfway up the Bosphorus on opposite shores, stand facing each other. These, built by the

Turks, and the other earlier fortresses on the hills near the Black Sea, are military installations indicating the strategic importance of the Bosphorus in every age. Viewed from the Sea of Marmara end, where the historic city looks most impressive, the Bosphorus appears like a small bay. The rest of the 30 kilometre-long stretch up to the Black Sea appears as consecutive lakes. The first suspension bridge across the Bosphorus was completed in 1973 to celebrate the 50th anniversary of the Turkish Republic and the second one in 1988. Only an aerial-view shows that the Bosphorus is actually a strait. The Bosphorus is a unique "sea-river". The less

*Fatih Sultan Mehmet Bridge on the Bosphorus.*

saline waters of the Black Sea flow towards the Sea of Marmara on the surface, while below the surface, there is another current flowing in the opposite direction. Due to these strong surface currents and the lack of roads, there were few settlements along its shores up until the end of the last century. In the 19th century, besides the small villages, imperial palaces and the summer residences of the wealthy as well as foreign embassies started to appear along its shores. Today, the residential districts along the shores, served by modern roads, suspension bridges and ferry boats, are included within the borders of the metropolis. The strait, which was a river alley in the Ice Age, has a rich marine fauna. It has an average depth of 50 metres and a maximum depth of 112 metres. Different species of fish migrate through these waters seasoally. The name "Bosphorus" is derived from mythology and it means the "Bull's Passage". Since it is an easily traversed passage, it facilitated the developmente of trade and other relations between civilizations in Asia and Europe. The Bosphorus, its extension, the Golden Horn and the peninsula on which the historic city of Istanbul developed, have been the most sought after location in the world during the last 2,500 years. The campaign of the Argonauts to the Black Sea is the first mythological story about the Bosphorus. In the 6th century B.C., the Persian armies, in order to cross the Bosphorus easily, tied their boats together side by side, thus forming the first bridge on the Bosphorus. During the "Retreator Ten Thousands" of Xenophon in the 5th century B.C., their race for Byzantium was mentioned as a very important event.

# THE BEYLERBEYI PALACE

The palace was built on the site of an older wooden mansion between the years 1861-1865. Western motifs along with Turkish and eastern motifs were used to decorate the building. It has two sections: the Harem (for ladies) and the Selamlik (for men). Including the ground floor, the mansion is three-storeyed and has twenty-six rooms and six halls. The small pavilions located at each end of the long quay were for recreation. There are gardens and terraces with pools behind the building. The Stable Pavilion here is the finest example of its kind, and the pavilions nearby were built before it. The large mansion has a well-arranged garden and a richly ornamented marble exterior. The large hall in the centre section of the palace has a pool and a spiral staircase. The different artistic styles displayed in the decorations of the hall give it a striking appearance. During its golden days, the mansion was used during the summers and also to accommodate visiting state dignitaries. It has been preserved in its original condition.

## VILLA BOSPHORUS

Near the imperial seaside mansion is Villa Bosphorus which is an excellent spot to rest and shop during the tours of the Asian shores of the Bosphorus or during a boat ride. It is a distinguished shopping center with its well-arranged gardens and streets. High-quality jewellery, leather and suede apparel and Turkish souvenirs are offered tourists in the 3 stores VILLA BOSPHORUS, SULTAN LEATHER, ASIATIC BAZAAR.

*Villa Bosphorus in Beylerbeyi, an excellent shopping center on the Asian shore.*

*The Beylerbeyi Palace.*

*The Göksu stream.*

*Anadolu Hisari, or Anatolian Fortress.*

# ANADOLU HISARI
# (The Anatolian Fortress)

The Küçüksü Pavilion and the fortress are situated by a park on the Asian shores of the Bosphorus. It is quite a small fortress built between 1390 and 1391, before the European Fortress on the opposite shore, by Sultan Bayazid, to control the traffic on the Bosphorus, and as a step in the preparations for the final seige of Istanbul. A street passes through this picturesque fortress, situated at a strategic location by the sea, next to a stream that drains into the Bosphorus. There are old wooden houses resting against the small towers of the fortress.

The Kanlica district, which comes after the fortress, is famous for its yoghurt and seaside cafés. The Asian tower of the new "Fatih Bridge" is also situated here.

# SARIYER

Sariyer is the last stop of the half-day cruises on the Bosphorus. It is also a summer resort which offers a relaxed atmosphere, seaside restaurants and woods in the vicinity.

The last residential district after Sariyer along the Bosphorus on the European side, is the Rumeli Kavaği district which may be reached either by boat or by car. The rest of the land along the shore after the Rumeli Kavaği district is a restricted area since it belongs to the military. The Anadolu Kavaği district on the Asian side is the last stop for the ferry boats and it is a small fishing village famous for its reasonably priced restaurants.

The beaches in Kilyos, which is only 25 km. from Istanbul, are patronized by lovers of the sea. Accomodation in the village includes a motel and pensions.

*The Tarabya Bay and the Tarabya Hotel.*

*An old mansion.*

*The Sadberk Hanim Museum at Büyükdere.*

*The fishing village of Rumeli Kavaği*

*Leander's tower at sunset.*

*A view of Istanbul from Üsküdar.*

# THE LEANDER'S TOWER

Western sources erroneously state that this is the spot where Leander drowned as he was trying to swim across the strait to be with his lover, Hera. Actually, this incident took place in the Dardanelles, not in teh Bosphorus.

This rather small structure, known as the Maiden's tower (Kiz Kulesi), stands on a small islet and has become one of the symbols of Istanbul. Through the ages, it was used as a watch-tower, a lighthouse and a customs house. Today, it serves as a landmark for ships entering the Bosphorus, and has not changed since the last century.

# THE PRINCES' ISLANDS

The archipelago known as the Princes' Islands consists of nine various sized islands in the Sea of Marmara and is only an hour away by boat from the pier in the Golden Horn. It is known that during the Byzantine era there were many monasteries here. Some of these were used as imperial summer residences and some were used to house the exiled.

Heybeli Ada is the second largest islands in the archipelago. A small church (the last Byzantine structure built before the fall of Byzantium) dedicated to the Virgin is situated in the inner courtyard of the Naval School on the island. In the beginning of the 19th century, when steamboats started serving the islands, the population of the islands started to increase. Halki Palace Hotel on the Heybeli island is the oldest hotel in Istanbul. Fully renovated in 1994, the hotel is the best place away from the crowded downtown for perfect rest, swimming and jogging.

The four larger islands are popular summer resorts with ideal picnic areas and beautiful beaches. The islands are heavily populated from May until the end of September, and then become almost desolate in the winter. Scheduled ferry boats serve the islands from the mainland. Throughout the summer and especially on weekends, private boats, yachts and sail-boats anchor in the beautiful coves around every island. Motor vehicles are not allowed on the islands, the shores of which are lined by seaside mansions, beaches and picnic areas. Horse-drawn carriages are the only means of transportation.

Woods and parks cover the hills on the islands while residences line the northern shores that face the Asian side of Istanbul.

The first island seen from the ferry boat after leav-

*The Islands with beaches opened to the public.*

*Merit Halki Palace Hotel located on Heybeli Ada, the second largest island in the archipelago. The building was renovated in 1944. Scheduled ferry rides allow transport to the island.*

ing the pier is the conical shaped, desolate Hayirsiz Ada. Next to it is the flat Yassi Ada. Although there are military installations on this island, projects are underway to use them for tourism.

Kinali Ada is the first inhabited island with a beautiful bay in the back, and with beaches opened to the public. Burgaz, with its rocky beaches, comes after Kinali. There are watersports clubs on the island.

By the square next to the pier at Heybeli Ada and between its two hills, are the buildings of the Naval Schools. Beaches occupy its two beautiful coves. The large buildings of the orthodox Church were used as a school for the monks in the old days. Halki Palace Hotel on the island is the oldest hotel in Istanbul. Between Burgaz Ada and Heybeli Ada is a small private island called Kasik Adasi (Spoon Island) due to its shape.

Bayakada is the largest, the most popular and the most famous island in the archipelago. It takes two hours to go around the island (the complete tour) in a horsedrawn carriage. This island with high hills, has two public beaches, one of which is situated in an unusually beautiful cove.

The most popular ride on the island follows a course between tha mansions in wellkept gardens and through the forests on the hills (the half-tour). Unlike the heavily populated residential areas near ideal harbours for small boats. Fish restaurants and cafés line the seashore near the pier, and there are a few hotels and pensions on the island. On weekends and holidays, people crowd the island for a picnic and to swim. The small promontory on the side of the island facing Heybeli Ada is covered with pine forests and it is a very popular recreation area.

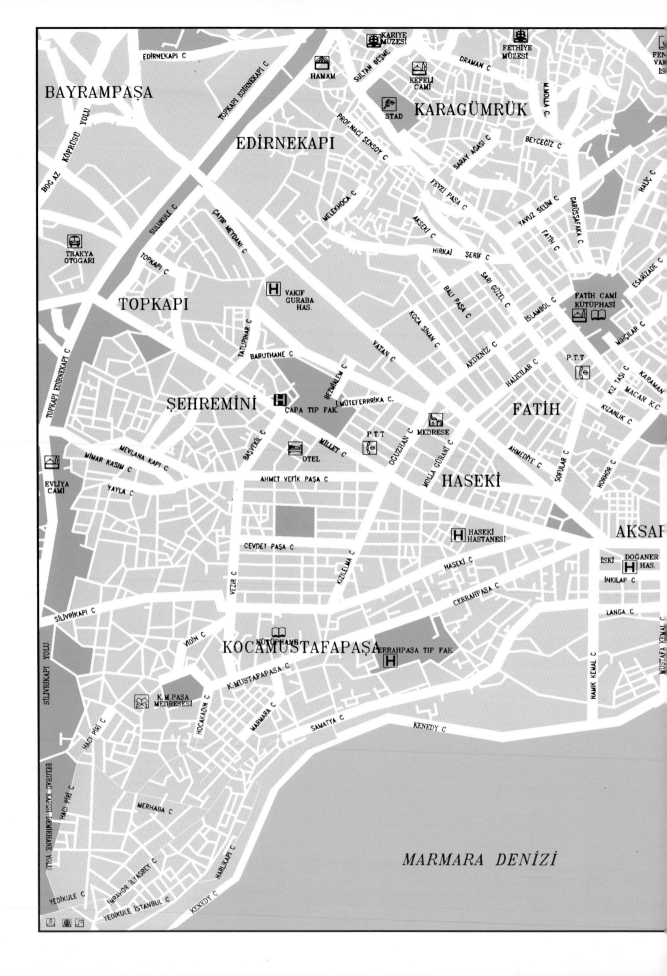

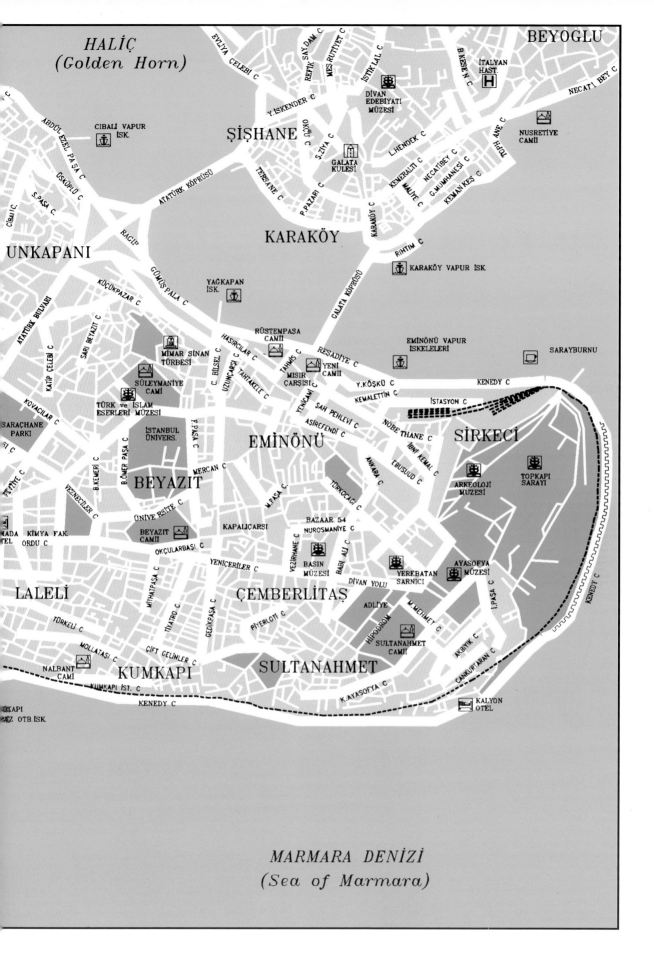

# INDEX